GROWING VEGETABLE IN CONTAINER

A DIY GUIDE TO GROWING VEGGIE AT HOME

STEVE MUFIA

Text Copyright © 2018 STEVE MUFIA

All rights reserved. No part of this guide may be reproduced in any form without permission in writing from the publisher except in the case of brief quotations embodied in critical articles or reviews.

Legal & Disclaimer

The content or information contained in this book is not designed to replace or take the place of any form of medical or professional advice; and is not meant to replace the need for independent medical, financial, legal or other professional advice or services, as may be required. The content or information in this book has been provided for educational and entertainment purposes only.

The content or information contained in this book is from sources deemed reliable, and it is accurate to the best of the author's knowledge, information, and belief. However, the author cannot guarantee its accuracy and validity and cannot be held liable for any errors and omissions. Further changes are periodically made to this book as and when needed. Where appropriate and necessary, you must consult a professional (including but not limited to your doctor, attorney, financial advisor or such other professional advisor) before using any of the suggested remedies, techniques, or information in this book.

Upon using the content or information contained in this book, you agree not to hold the author responsible for any damages, costs, and expenses, including any legal fees, potentially resulting from the application of any of the information provided in this book. This disclaimer applies to any loss, damages or injury caused by the use and application, whether directly or indirectly, of any advice or information presented, whether for breach of contract, tort, negligence, personal injury, criminal intent, or under any other cause of action.

You agree to accept all risks of using the information presented in this book.

You agree that by continuing to read this book, where appropriate and necessary, you shall consult a professional (including but not limited to your doctor, attorney, or financial advisor or such other advisor as needed) before using any of the suggested remedies, techniques, or information in this book.

Table of Contents

INTRODUCTION 6

CHAPTER ONE 9

GROWING VEGETABLE IN A CONTAINER 9

CHAPTER TWO 14

All About Essential Gardening Tools and Equipment.. 14

CHAPTER THREE 20

TYPES OF VEGETABLES SUITABLE TO BE GROWN IN CONTAINERS.. 20

CHAPTER FOUR 23

TYPE OF CONTAINER SUITABLE FOR GROWING VEGETABLES.. 23

CHAPTER FIVE 27

PREPARING YOUR SOIL 27

CHAPTER SIX 31

HOW TO GROW CARROTS IN CONTAINERS....... 31

CHAPTER SEVEN 39

HOW TO GROW TOMATOES IN CONTAINERS ... 39

CHAPTER EIGHT 45

HOW TO GROW LETTUCE IN A CONTAINER 45

CHAPTER NINE 50

HOW TO GROW POTATOES IN CONTAINERS..... 50

CHAPTER TEN.. 58

HOW TO GROW CABBAGE IN CONTAINERS 58

CHAPTER ELEVEN.. 64

HOW TO GROW SPINACH IN CONTAINERS 64

CONCLUSION 69

Check Out Other Books 71

INTRODUCTION

Lack of space to plant your favorite fruit trees, vegetables, and herbs should not prevent you from having a garden that will yield fresh produce for you and your family to enjoy. Most families that live in apartments, condominium units, or places that don't offer a big enough space to create a regular garden turn to container gardening. Although a container garden has many similarities with a regular garden, you may need to exert some extra work regarding proper care and maintenance.

Aside from having fresh and chemical-free produce, there are other benefits that container gardening can provide. It can help relieve stress after long hours of work. Your container garden can also provide a relaxing atmosphere, an eco-friendly house decoration, and an abundant supply of oxygen.

There has never been a more suitable time to learn about vegetable gardening than now. It ticks all the right boxes. It saves money and satisfies our pleasure-seeking appetites. With vegetable gardening, you have several choices to grow interesting flavors in the comfort of your home.

Why is it important to eat vegetables?

Vegetable consumption has several health benefits as it is recommended to be included as part of our daily diet. Regular consumption of vegetables helps to reduce the risk associated with some chronic diseases. Vegetables help to provide important nutrients needed for health and maintenance of the body system.

Nutrients

Vegetables are great sources of low fat and calories, and they do not contain cholesterol. They are great sources of vitamin A, vitamin C, dietary fiber, potassium, and folic acid. All these essential nutrients work together to make the body healthy.

Health benefits

Eating a diet rich in vegetables may help to reduce the risk of cardiovascular disease.

Eating a diet rich in vegetables may help to protect against certain types of cancers.

Eating a diet rich in vegetables which contains a high amount of fiber may help to reduce the risk of obesity, and type 2 diabetes. Blood pressure is also lowered when you eat potassium-rich vegetables.

These and much more are the reasons why you need to start your vegetable garden right in your home by planting your favorite vegetable plant. In this book, we would succinctly discuss tips on how to conveniently plant vegetable in containers. So, at the end of this book, you will be able to plant vegetable of your choice in your home conveniently.

CHAPTER ONE

GROWING VEGETABLE IN A CONTAINER

There are several media of growing vegetables in the home, and the container grown vegetable is one of the easiest. Growing vegetable in containers comes with lots of advantage as one gets to experience the flavor and freshness of home-grown vegetables.

Here's a little-known secret: Most vegetables grown in containers are known to flourish well and if you carefully select the right plants, you can start up a vegetable container garden of your own whereby you grew a considerable amount of food in just a few containers!

Vegetables planted in containers should be done the same way you would plant in the garden. Depending on the type of vegetable you intend to grow, you can either plant seeds directly in your containers, or you transplant from a garden center.

Vegetable crops such as carrots, beans, radishes, and spinach, can be planted from seeds and sown directly in the container.

Regardless of whether you are directly planting the seeds or transplanting, you need to adequately water the container before planting. Completely soak the potting mix and leave it for a few hours to allow the excess water to drain.

Plant seeds in excess because some seeds might not be viable enough, then you thin accordingly as they germinate. For transplants, you can set the stems at the same level they were in their pot. With the exception of tomatoes, you can trim off the lower leaves and plant deep into the soil in the container.

After planting, gently water to help the seeds or transplants settle. You could also practice mulching even in your vegetable containers by using compost, leaf mold, straw or any other similar material. This helps to preserve moisture and retain nutrients in the soil.

Picking a Spot for Your Container

Most container-grown vegetables thrive well in full sun (at least 6 hours of direct sunlight daily). Tomatoes, peppers, and other disease prone variety stay healthiest when placed in an open spot with enough air circulation.

If you live in a cold climate, it would be good to situate your vegetable containers garden near a south-facing wall.

If you live in a warmer climate, try to avoid setting your vegetable container garden on a cement enclosure. This is because it may get too warm for optimum growth.

What Types of Soil Should I Use in Container?

While your vegetables don't really care so much about the kind of container you put them in, they do care much about the type of soil you put in the container.

Your vegetable container garden will thrive well in organic potting mixes as it's also applicable to other types of container gardens. Just before you purchase your soil from the nursery, ask for the soil mixture designed specifically for use in larger outdoor containers.

Alternatively, you can cut cost by getting your vegetable container garden mix by yourself. Mix equal parts of peat moss, potting soil, and clean sand. Fill your containers with your soil mix within an inch or two of the container top.

This will guide you to knowing how much potting mix you'll need:

- 3 pints of soil per 6-inch pot

- $3^1/_2$ gallons of mix per 12-inch pot
- $6^1/_2$ gallons of mix per 20-inch pot

Care Guide

The most important cultural practice to be done in your container vegetable garden is watering. Ensure you properly and consistently water your container garden to prevent your potting mix from drying out.

You could make your watering easier by installing a drip-irrigation system which automatically irrigates your vegetables.

Another cultural practice to do is fertilizer application, and this can be started around a month after planting. Apply water-soluble fertilizer to your vegetables in the right proportion (follow the directions on the package). Also, don't leave out the weed and pest control. You can practice weeding by simply uprooting the weeds with your hand.

Harvest Tips

Harvest is the reward for all your several weeks of labor and this is what we are all looking forward to. You only need a few tips to get it right at this stage. Handpick your vegetables from the container garden as soon as they reach your desired size. Most vegetables flourish when they are harvested early and frequently.

At the end of the planting season, pour out your container soil and use it for compost. It is not advisable to reuse the same soil year in year out as it can spread infections and cause insect infestations. Scrub the container thoroughly to remove all soil. After pouring out the soil, rinse your container in a bleach solution of 1 to 10 parts of water followed by rinsing with clean water and store in a dry spot.

CHAPTER TWO

All About Essential Gardening Tools and Equipment

The right tools always make your work easier. You need to have the right tools if you want to make container gardening more fun.

The Tools You Need

You can purchase these tools at garden centers or other stores. You can also try online shops that sell garden tools and order from them.

Trowel

A trowel or soil scoop is probably the most helpful tool that you need for your container garden. It can help you fill your containers with soil in a jiffy or if you need to mix your potting soil. You use a trowel when you need to transfer your plant from one container to the other. If you have small children in your house, then it is advisable to buy a trowel that has a rounded or almost rounded tip to prevent possible injury.

Scrub Brush

A scrub brush can help you remove soil, salt deposits, and moss off your planters or containers and keep your garden neat and fresh all the time.

Wheelbarrow or Hand Truck

A wheelbarrow or a hand truck can help you transport your containers to the spot that you want them to occupy. If you plan to have your container garden in your home, then it is advisable to prepare them outside (to avoid creating a mess inside your home). You can transport your garden using your wheelbarrow when you have finished putting your plants in their respective containers.

Hose-end Bubbler

A hose-end bubbler is an attachment that must be screwed at the end of your hose. It helps soften the water flow when you need to water your plants and prevents any soil washout. You can also use a metal hose-end extension when watering your hard-to-reach containers and hanging plants.

Watering Can

It is recommended to use a watering can when you need to water your indoor plants. You can also add liquid fertilizer to your watering can when it is time to feed some to your plants.

Mister

The container garden in your house requires extra humidity, and a mister can help you provide the needed humidity. A small hand spray is enough to do the job.

Pruning Shears

Dead leaves can make your container garden look dull and lifeless. It is best to remove the dead leaves right away using the pruning shears. You can also use your shears when it is time to harvest your produce.

Artificial Lighting

If you have decided to put your container garden inside your house, then you need artificial lighting for your garden. The artificial light can give your plants the amount of light they need in the absence of natural light coming from the sun. Plants have chlorophyll which makes photosynthesis possible. Photosynthesis produces food and energy for the plants, but there will be no photosynthesis if chlorophyll won't get enough light. You need light to help your plants thrive.

It is recommended that for every 18" by 18" garden patch, you need to provide artificial lights of around 100 watts. You can also choose CFL bulbs, or you can ask your garden supplier for any cheaper alternative that can provide the required amount of light for your plants to grow and stay healthy.

Saucer for your Pot

You may also want to use saucers for your pots. The saucer will collect the water that runs out from your containers. Plastic saucers are the most ideal because they don't break easily or leave stains underneath.

Choosing the Right Gardening Tools

In choosing your gardening tools, it is advisable to try them out first before buying them. See if the weight is just right for you, i.e. not too light and not too heavy. It should be easy and comfortable to hold. Choose the size that fits most of your garden projects. The grip should be just right so that the tool won't slip from your hand.

Garden tools are made from different materials. If you want something light, then you can choose the tools made from plastic, carbon, and aluminum. If you want something easy to clean and can slide into the soil without trouble, then stainless steel tools are the most suitable choice. If you are looking for something strong and will last for a long time, then solid forged steel tools are the ones you need.

Being expensive or sophisticated does not mean that the tool will be able to give you the results you want to achieve. It is best to choose something that is comfortable, durable, and easy to use and maintain.

A gardening tool that comes with interchangeable heads is also a good choice, but it can be expensive. Try to purchase something within your budget, especially if you only have limited funds. If your budget can cover the cost of the tool with interchangeable heads, then buy it. Always choose the tools that are durable, and most of the time, the ones made by reputable companies are the best choice.

Choosing the right tools can make gardening easier and more enjoyable.

Proper Tool Care and Maintenance

It is not hard to care for your tools, but it does require a bit of your time. You need to clean your tools after using them. It is important to let them dry first before storing them away.

Apply boiled linseed oil on your tools to prevent rusting. Gardeners have been using the said oil for many years. You can also treat the wooden handle of your tool with linseed oil when the handle has no more protective coating.

Take note that the commercially available boiled linseed oil has an added small amount of solvent to prevent it from hardening inside the can. After applying the oil to your tool, it is wise to let the oil dry out completely (which usually takes about 24 hours) before using your tool again.

Make sure to keep your tools indoors. It is recommended to hang them so they won't touch the wall or floor of the storage as well as anything that can make them come in contact with moisture.

You can make your tools work for a long time if you take good care of them.

CHAPTER THREE

TYPES OF VEGETABLES SUITABLE TO BE GROWN IN CONTAINERS

Vegetables do great when planted in containers as well as the garden. Here are some commonly planted container vegetables as well as the basic instructions you will need in order to grow a certain variety of vegetable.

Note: The planting instructions suggested here are for optimal growth.

- Carrots: Direct seed into a container with a depth of about 2 to 5 gallons.

- Tomatoes: Transplant one plant per 5-gallon container.

- Cucumber: Two transplants per 5-gallon container.

- Cabbage: One transplant per 5-gallon container.

- Spinach: Direct seed into 1-gallon container. Thin to 3 inches apart.

- Pepper: Two transplants per 5-gallon container.

- Lettuce: Direct seed or transplant into 1-gallon container.

- Radishes: Direct seed into 2-gallon. Thin to 3 inches apart.

- Swiss Chard: Transplant or direct seed - 4 plants per container of 5-gallon.

- Kohlrabi: Direct seed into a 5-gallon container.

- Peas: Direct seed into 5-gallon container.

- Beets: Direct seed into a 2-5-gallon window box.

- Onion: Direct seed into a large container. Thin to 2 inches between plants.

- Summer Squash: Transplant or direct seed, 2 plants per 5-gallon container.

- Broccoli: 1 transplant per 5-gallon container.

- Eggplant: 1 transplant per 5-gallon container.

- Green Beans: Sow into a 5-gallon container or window box.

- Winter Squash: Plant directly from seed ensuring a plant per 5-gallon container.

There are other vegetable types that could be planted in containers but these are the most commonly planted and they are known to thrive well in containers.

CHAPTER FOUR

TYPE OF CONTAINER SUITABLE FOR GROWING VEGETABLES

Plant containers usually come in many styles and materials. When it comes to choosing the containers to use for your container garden, consider the maximum size of the plants that you want to grow. That way, you don't need to go through the painstaking process of transferring your plants when they begin to outgrow their current containers.

Choosing the Right Size

Gardeners can choose clay, wood, or plastic containers. There are commercially available pots that come in different styles and designs to suit the gardener's preference. You can also recycle some of your containers or other things in your house and turn them into awesome pots to house your plants.

Bigger containers are the better choice if you intend to grow large plants. If your container has enough space for the roots to grow, then your plants won't get cramped. It is also easier to water the plant and add fertilizer when needed.

The depth or width of the container is crucial for the vegetables. You can grow radishes or carrots in a container with a narrow width, but make sure that it is deep enough to accommodate the growing vegetable beneath the soil.

A half wine barrel is an ideal container for growing lots of vegetables. It is inexpensive and can be a good addition to your interior décor. You only need to use your creativity to the fullest to get the look that you want to achieve. You can put a maximum of two tomato plants, ten heads of lettuce, or two cucumbers in the barrel half. The barrel can be purchased at garden nurseries and centers.

Don't put small plants in big containers because they look unappealing and ridiculous. Choose the size wisely and use your best judgment in estimating the possible growth of your plant.

Choosing the Right Material

The material of the container affects the frequency of watering you need for your plants. The material also determines how long your container would last. Containers made of clay or other porous materials dry out faster than wood or plastic containers.

You need to water your plants more frequently, especially during windy or hot weather, if you are using clay containers. Wood containers will eventually rot in the long run so make sure to choose rot-resistant woods like redwood and cedar. Plastic containers may become brittle over time, but they can last for a long time.

Take note that wood containers that were treated with chemicals to preserve their beauty are not suitable for growing your edible plants. The soil might absorb the chemicals and transfer the chemical to your produce, making it potentially unsafe for consumption.

There are also polypropylene bags that you can use for your container garden. Polypropylene is a breathable fabric that promotes the right aeration for your plants and prevents overwatering. These bags come in a variety of sizes and depths to accommodate the plant that you intend to grow.

Unusual and Inexpensive Containers

You can actually use any kind of planter for your container garden. As mentioned earlier, you can recycle and use anything in your house as containers or planters.

For your hanging plants, you can use old baskets that you no longer use. Make sure that your baskets have adequate drainage and properly supported by a chain, rope, wire, or what have you. A full hanging old basket with soil and plants can be quite heavy, and the unsupported handle of the basket may suddenly snap. If you are going to use an old basket, then you need to support it properly.

You can use tea kettles, cookie tins, basins, and other things that you don't use anymore but can hold your plants. Punch enough holes for the drainage, add some soil, and put your vegetable or herb. Practice proper care and maintenance, and you will be harvesting fresh produce in no time.

CHAPTER FIVE

PREPARING YOUR SOIL

Although traditional gardening and container gardening may have some similarities. Understand that the soil for container gardening needs to be well aerated. It should have proper drainage and can retain the moisture that the plants need to survive.

No matter how good your garden soil is, it is recommended not to use it alone in a container garden. When used alone, both aeration and drainage are affected which results in poor plant growth or no growth at all.

Soils used for container gardening should be modified to meet the required aeration and drainage. Soils that gardeners commonly use for containers are often referred to as artificial media or soilless because they contain no dirt. They are usually composed of various materials such as vermiculite, peat moss, coir fiber, and bark.

You need to slightly moisten the soil before planting if you prefer to use artificial media. Fill your container with soil, pour enough water, and lightly fluff the soil to dampen it evenly.

You can use garden soil, but you need to modify it first. An ideal soil based mix is one part each of garden soil, perlite, and peat moss.

Advantages and Disadvantages of Soilless and Modified Garden Soil

The modified garden soil is heavier than soilless media. It can provide the needed weight which allows the containers to keep upright during windy days especially if your garden is located outside your house. Soilless media may not be able to provide the needed weight to keep the pots in place.

Modified garden soil cannot guarantee that you will be able to get a disease-free soil for your garden. Your garden soil may contain weed seeds, harmful organisms, and pests that can harm your plants later on. Soilless media doesn't have such things, and it is completely safe.

The garden soil is a lot cheaper than soilless media. Modified garden soil doesn't dry out fast and can hold the nutrients longer.

In terms of aeration, soilless media is the more suitable soil to use. You can also stretch it and fill more containers by adding and mixing some modified garden soil in it. But, such practice may be risky because the garden soil could be infected with diseases. You can also reuse your soilless media year after year, provided that the plants that used the soil did not contaminate the soil with a disease. Using contaminated soil will only cause illness to your plants. Also, you may need to add fertilizer for added nutrients for your plants. It is also advisable to add compost.

Filling your Containers

When filling your containers with your chosen soil, avoid filling the container to the top. Allow a one-inch space between the rim of your container and the top of your soil. This will prevent the water from running over the edge.

Filling large containers is costly especially if you are using commercially prepared soil. To save some money, add some filler at the bottom of the container to take up space. Just make sure that the roots of your plants will not lose the space they need while growing. In cases where the roots might touch the bottom of the container, it is wise to fill the whole container with soil. If you happen to have miscalculations and your plant outgrows the original container, then you should transfer it to a bigger one while you still can. You can also give it to someone who can provide the right area and enough room to grow.

Non-biodegradable items can be used as fillers such as small plastic jugs, crushed aluminum cans, and other packaging. Line a piece of landscape fabric above the filler and begin adding your soil. The fabric will keep the soil from invading the area of the filler while allowing the water to pass through without trouble.

Begin planting if there is already enough soil to hold the plant. Finish adding the soil until you achieve the required space between the soil and the rim of the pot. Use your garden tools when preparing your container garden to make things easier. Always keep your tools handy and in tip-top shape. Don't strain your back and use your hand truck when transporting your filled containers.

Soil preparation can make or break your container garden. It is advisable to use the soilless media because it is safer and more suitable for your container garden.

CHAPTER SIX

HOW TO GROW CARROTS IN CONTAINERS

Starting up a garden can be inspired by carrots of any type or color. There are many unusual colors of carrot, such as Purple Haze that is often seen in the stores. The white, yellow and red carrots look beautiful too but they are not often found in the stores. Planting carrots require little skill, minimal effort and minimal care. With spring planting effort, you can be sure of a great harvest in the late summer. Carrots are high in beta-carotene, vitamin C, vitamin B6, calcium, and niacin.

Long ago, in the days when everyone had a backyard garden, carrots were always multicolored and it was a normal thing, but somewhere along the way, people decided that carrots should be orange and the other colors were no longer known for several decades.

Now, with the advantages that people derive from eating local organic food, the other colors of carrots are coming back to the limelight. If you shop at a farmers markets or in the speciality markets, you may see some carrots that are purple in color or maybe a bag of mixed color rainbow carrots.

There is a creative idea for planting; buy a seeder, then before planting, mix some of the purple carrot seed pack and the multicoloured carrot seed pack in a dish, then mix them together, put them in the seeder and start planting. This makes it a super fun and creative way to grow and pick the carrots, especially for people that love colors because you never know which color is going to grow out next, it could be white, red, purple, yellow or even orange. There are so many delicious and beautiful types of carrot that you can grow. You can use the harvest on a summer vegetable platter in a gorgeous rainbow and amaze your guests.

Soil Needs

Carrots prefer a loose and light soil with some perlite mixed in it. This makes it easier for the roots to grow long and straight down. The ideal pH for them is 6.0 to 6.8. If you are planting in a small number of tubs or containers, then it is advisable to buy good quality bagged potting soil for vegetables in containers. The carrot plant will struggle to grow through a dense or rocky soil. With a dense or rocky soil, the carrot plants will be stumpier, shorter and sometimes growing in awkward directions with two or three roots. If their roots grow into a rock or are grown in rocky soil, then the carrots sprouts will grow around them, become crooked and bent in awkward ways. Digging up existing garden soil to put in a container is not safe for growing carrots, it is usually too dense and will be very hard packed. It is an unfavorable environment for the carrot seeds to sprout.

Type of Container

All varieties of carrots will grow well in any container that is a decent size and more than 12 inches in depth. Planting in a raised bed is a good method too. This method gives enough depth for carrots to grow. It's very likely that you'll be able to harvest them early enough. It takes 60 to 75 days to harvest carrot depending on the variety. They are a cool weather crop and prefer the cooler weather of spring and early fall, this is the reason why carrots can be grown well into the fall in most areas. They grow well in these zones. At regular intervals, you could keep planting new seeds as long as there are enough space and time before the winter is over. All you need to do to figure this out is subtract the "days to harvest" from the expected frost date in your area. This will let you know when to plant with enough time to see the seeds through to the harvest.

Planting

Carrot seeds are tiny and hard to manage. After spreading them on the soil they are quite hard to see, so it becomes difficult to know when you've planted the right amount. It's much possible to over plant a carrot container. If this happens and you accidentally plant too many seeds, do not panic, just leave it and allow them to sprout. Let them grow to about 1 inch to 2 inches tall, then carefully cut out the smaller sprouts with scissors. Don't pull them out because it may damage neighboring sprouts. The root will eventually die off and serve as manure to the soil, thereby allowing the stronger seedlings to grow. If the seeds are overcrowded, then none of them will grow large and healthy. You can plant approximately 4 seeds per square inch. This creates room for the larger ones to grow healthy and strong. This will not happen if the seeds are overcrowded.

Seed tape is a good way to simplify the task of planting the tiny little seeds but the setback is that only a few selected varieties are available in tape form.

There are other smaller variety of seeds that are in form of pellets. This simply means that each seed has been coated in an inert, organic clay material. This makes them much larger and easy to handle and they are very easy to see once sprinkled on the soil. The coating quickly dissolves in the rain and the seed sprouts normally. One package of seeds will go quite far and will be enough for 2 large 18 inches containers. It might be tempting to put more seeds because it gives a more beautiful carrot but it is important to resist doing this. Too many seeds in one container are not good. Once you've planted the pelleted seeds and covered them with a thin layer of soil, pat it down just a little. Then, use a gentle sprinkler to water them so as not to turn up the soil and disturb the seeds. Use a handheld hose wand with a soft spray or a watering can with small holes.

The number of days it takes to Sprout

They don't need too much water but it needs to be consistently moist. Keep them lightly watered but not too wet while they grow. The top few inches of soil should stay moist all the time. If there is no rain, keep them watered so that the surface doesn't dry and form a crust. It is important to keep the top few inches of soil moist until they sprout. Then, if the temperature outside is right, you should see sprouts popping up within 14 – 17 days. It is also important to know that the seeds will lie dormant, grow very slowly or stop growing completely right where they are if the temperature reduces after planting or isn't high enough to meet their ideal growing conditions to sprout. The optimum temperature required for their growth is a consistent 13 degrees Celsius or higher. They will resume growing as though nothing happened when the temperature rises into this range. They don't like to be too hot either. The seedlings begin to suffer when the temperature increases above 30 degrees Celsius. In about 60 – 75 days from planting you'll be able to start to pick the size of carrots you can use for dinner and snacks.

In some cases, as the carrots grow, it happens that the plant will push up out of the soil a little bit. This exposes the top end of the carrot (the shoulders) to the sun and causes it to turn green. This isn't unhealthy but it's just not very good looking. The way to solve this problem if it happens is to reserve a bit of soil in the bag and when you see the shoulders starting to show, just add a bit more soil to cover them up again to block out the sun.

Picking

When picking the carrots, select the ones with the largest, thickest greens and then gently pull them up. Sometimes they need a wiggle. Then wash or brush off the soil and enjoy. You won't even have to peel them, they'll have a deliciously irresistible, earthy flavor.

Briefly, here are instructions to get you going with learning how to grow carrots in containers or raised beds;

Carrot Facts Summary

- Very tiny seeds

- Easy to grow

- Cool weather crop

- Seeds sprout at about 13 degrees Celsuis

- Prefer loose, loamy soil
- pH of 6.0 to 6.8
- Nearly pest free when grown in containers

CHAPTER SEVEN

HOW TO GROW TOMATOES IN CONTAINERS

Tomatoes have been eagerly planted by many gardeners. Growing tomatoes in containers can either be the most satisfying or a very great disaster. Times come when there is nothing you can do to prevent failure in growing tomatoes. It could be due to bad weather, critter problems or late blight. However, to improve the chances for the growth of tomatoes, there are some things that you can do. Tomatoes may not be the easiest but they are surely one of the favorite plants to grow. A freshly picked tomato, still warm from the sun, is the closest a taste that is natural. In no particular order, the following steps can help you have success with growing tomatoes in container pots.

Use Really Big Containers

Using a very big container is one of the most important things you can do to ensure successful tomato growth, the bigger the size of the container the better. Unless it is a very small variety of tomato, one tomato plant will require at least a square foot pot or container but 2 square feet is better. A five-gallon bucket, the ones you get at restaurants, food factories or hardware stores are the perfect size for one tomato plant. A large size reusable grocery bag can also be used; it's also a perfect size.

Some people are extremely enthusiastic about tomatoes and grow them primarily for food and not for looks, so they put one plant per container (thereby they plant one stand per container with the exception of those using large containers, earth box or raised bed).

So many people suggest growing herbs and other plants in the same pot alongside the tomato, but it's hard enough to give tomatoes the amount of moisture they need consistently without bringing in other plants that will compete for the water. A good drainage is very essential, while you should also fill up the large container with a potting soil that is of good quality.

Add more water consistently but it must not be too much

Giving the tomato plant a consistent amount of water is the key to its successful growth. This can also be the biggest challenge for growing tomatoes in pots. The aim of doing this is to keep the soil moist, not wet. If there is too much water at the plant's roots, it will rot and if the water is too little, the plants will get weak and your tomatoes will have a blossom end rot.

When the amount of water is inconsistent, either it's too little or too much, there will be an exploding or at least cracking tomatoes. Using self-watering containers is the easiest way to deal with this, otherwise, you will have to check your tomatoes every day. Often times, in the heat of the summer or when it's hot and windy, watering is done twice a day. If conventional containers are being used and there is too much rain, you can protect your tomatoes by covering them or moving them into a sheltered area if they are small enough. Plants take up and use water more efficiently in the morning, so watering your tomato plants early in the morning helps to aid the successful growth of the tomato plant. The soil are to be watered not the plants, as wet leaves can encourage blight and fungus.

Feed Your Tomatoes

It is very critical that you feed your tomatoes. Not taking cognizance of this crucial step may be the biggest and most common error most people make when growing tomato plants. There is no nutrient in the most potting soil which is essential for growing almost anything in containers. However, it is important to check your potting soil to be sure that there is fertilizer mixed in. If your potting soil doesn't have fertilizer, you will need to add a slow release fertilizer and you must thoroughly mix it with your potting soil.

A diluted liquid fertilizer such as liquid kelp meal or a fish emulsion fertiliser can be used to water your tomato plants every week or every other week, depending on how industrious you are.

Let the Sun Shine on your tomato plant

Most people overestimate the amount of sun gotten by their plant. The key to a successful and healthy growth of container tomatoes should be considered before you even plant them. When choosing where to grow your tomatoes, you have to accurately figure out a place where they will get enough sun. Tomato plants will do well with 6 hours plus of the full sun, which is the bare minimum and 8 hours plus is better. You can either employ the use of a sun calculator or go out and check your tomato containers several times over the day and time how much sun they are getting. If your plants are not getting enough sun, move them to a place where they will. Throughout your growing season, always check the movement of the sun across the sky, a place that use to be a full sun area can be shaded during a critical part of the day. Truly, tomato plants love the sun but if they are not slowly acclimated, it can lead to the death of delicate seedlings. Ensure you harden off your tomato seedlings as too much early exposure to sun and wind can weaken or kill the small plants. Tomato plants also like heat, so don't put them outside before it gets really warm (nights 50°F) or be ready to move or protect them from the cold. Also, note that tomato plants can fail if it's too hot.

Plant Tomatoes Deeply

Most plants will not thrive if you plant them too deep into the container soil, however, tomato plants are different. Plant your tomatoes deeply so that roots will develop from stems that are underground and the tomato plants will be healthier and stronger. When planting a tomato seedling, a deep hole must be dug so that most of the tomato plant is covered by soil, though you must ensure there are leaves above the soil level. All the leaves and branches below the soil line must be removed. If the pot or container is not deep enough to sink the tomato deeply, it should be if you use the appropriate type, you can also lay the plant on its side and cover it with the potting soil that way. A choice of good tomato varieties must be made because there are a lot of bad tomatoes out there, even some heirlooms are mealy and tasteless, and so make sure you are planting tomatoes that are of a good variety.

CHAPTER EIGHT

HOW TO GROW LETTUCE IN A CONTAINER

Lettuce is one of the vegetables that are very easy to grow in pots and it can even be grown in a small container. This crispy salad green called lettuce is healthy and continuously productive; it also has many qualities that make it good for the health. It is rich in water, vitamins, fibre and minerals such as calcium, potassium, sodium and magnesium. Lettuce is a perfect meal for those who have intestinal transit problems and also contributes to the smooth functioning of the nervous system.

You can start to harvest lettuce in about 8 weeks after planting for most of the varieties. It is very easy to grow and productive, it is similar to spinach. The most exciting part is that you don't need a lot of space to grow lettuce.

Requirements for growing lettuce in a container;

Choosing a Pot

Almost all the lettuce varieties grow well in pots because their shallow roots don't need deep soil. They thrive well in wide and shallow containers. Adequate drainage holes must be in the bottom of the pot and should be at least 6 inches deep. You can use any material for pots such as clay, plastic or terracotta pots.

However, in warm climates, if you're growing lettuce in a container, grow it in clay pots and plant heat-resistant varieties. Lettuce is a crop that grows in cold seasons and in most of the regions growing lettuce in pots or containers, it is possible from spring to fall. It is very easy to cultivate the lettuce from seeds or from seedlings. If you want to grow it from seeds, you can directly buy the seedlings from a nearby nursery. If you want to have a continuous harvest, practice successive planting, sowing seeds in every two weeks throughout the growing season. When the weather starts to heat up during summer, the lettuce tends to bolt and to reduce this tendency, keep your potted lettuce plant in a cool spot and provide proper shade.

Spacing

You can grow lettuce in a small space in your container garden. In doing this, you are likely to harvest your lettuce plants regularly; trying "Cut and Come Again" method. If you do this, you don't need to care much about spacing. Sow seeds densely and thin out the seedlings as they grow picking young, tender leaves regularly. Keep the plants 4-6 inches apart (depending on the size of the leaves you want to cultivate). However, more spacing is required for head lettuce than leaf lettuce and the planting depth must be increased to 8 inches.

Position

The lettuce requires more sunlight in cooler zones though it can be grown easily in a partially shaded area. If you're growing lettuce in a warm climate where the sun is very high, try to place the pot in a place that receives only a few hours of morning sun. During the hottest hours of the day especially in the afternoon, it is recommended to create a shade for the plant to prevent the drying of the soil, as lettuce prefers slightly moist soil constantly. Also, move the container in a cool spot when the temperature rises as lettuce are heat sensitive.

Soil

A mix of good quality soil which has plenty of organic matter such as peat and compost should be used for growing healthy lettuce. You can also add well-rotted manure or compost. The soil you use must be loamy and well-drained and should not hold water too much.

Watering

You may need to water frequently in shallow pots so that the plant will not dry out completely. Ensure that you do not only keep the soil slightly moist but also avoid overwatering the container of growing lettuce because overwatering can kill the plants due to root rot.

Fertilizer

A single or double application of fertilizer is usually all that is needed to boost the production because lettuce plants mature quickly. Before you fertilize, wait for a few weeks to allow the seedlings to establish. You can use a granular balanced fertilizer such as 10-10-10 to fertilize lettuce plant; liquid fertilizer can also be used for a quick boost. Ensure you follow the instructions provided by the manufacturer when applying fertilizer as both over and under fertilization can be harmful to the plant.

Pests and Diseases

Lettuce grown in containers is easily infested by pest and diseases, so they need to be protected from leaf-eating insects. However, if the plants are healthy, there are fewer chances of infestation of pests or diseases. Mildew, rot, leaf spot and a variety of bacterial infections are common diseases that can attack lettuce. Pests and insects that can cause damage to the plant include caterpillars, aphids, cutworms, maggots and beetles.

Harvesting

Once the lettuce leaves have reached the height of 4-6 inches which is the baby green size perfect for cut and come again method or according to your desired size, either pick the outer leaves individually or harvest them by cutting the leaves off 1 inch (2-3 cm) from above the base or crown. You must be careful not to cut into or below the crown or else your plant will die. When you do this, the plant will grow back and you'll be able to harvest it again. It's equally possible to pick your lettuce leaves before maturity, all you need do is to remove the outer leaves which can be useful for preparing salads while you allow the centre leaves to keep growing.

CHAPTER NINE

HOW TO GROW POTATOES IN CONTAINERS

A native potato that has simply been harvested out of the soil is a tremendous treat and potatoes are quite easy to grow organically in containers. Like tomatoes, the style and texture of recent potatoes are totally different to those you get from the shop. By growing your own, you may furthermore have the chance to plant uncommon varieties that are arduous to search out.

The Pros and Cons of Container Potatoes

There are many blessings to growing potatoes in containers instead of within the ground. Chief among them is that it's easier to shield the plants from the critters that like to eat them. Plus, you do not have to create additional house within the garden or worry about the excessive amount of weeds.

Container potatoes are an extremely fun project to try and do with children. The plant grows surprisingly quick and turns out a good yield. Besides, most children get pleasure from eating potatoes anyway, and they will love those they grow themselves even more.

The only real disadvantage to growing potatoes in containers is that you need to figure out how to water it constantly. It's vital to keep your soil moist, not wet, but damp. If you keep the soil moist and water deeply, you will definitely have a good potato harvest.

The Gardening Supplies You Need

Here are some things you will need for you to plant potatoes in containers:

- Seed potatoes

- Container

- Potting soil

- Fertilizer

- Sun and water

The Seed Potatoes

You can grow potatoes from "seed" potatoes. These potatoes haven't been sprayed to prevent their seeds from budding; therefore, they are prepared for new growth. Seed potatoes are out there from nurseries or speciality. You can obtain them from organic growers within your vicinity that features a nice choice of fascinating varieties.

You can additionally grow potatoes from organic potatoes from the shop. Ensure they have not been sprayed earlier and you merely have to allow them to sprout in a very cool, dark place.

The Container

Potatoes can be grown in any large containers, from giant pots or nursery containers to huge garbage cans. Even trash baggage or stacks of tires can do, although you have to use caution concerning these, as the sun could have huge effects on them. Also, the jury remains out on the potential toxicity of some plastics and rubber, which could leach into the soil because the material breaks down.

Another nice possibility is to plant potatoes in a very "potato abode." it's a home-brewed box created with wood planks that you simply build up because the plants grow and you add a lot of soil. This is often a reasonable vertical farming technique that may maximize your potato yield within a limited amount of space.

Whatever container you make use of for planting your potato, ensure that it has a good drainage system. If it doesn't, try and create one for it by making holes within the bottom.

Smart Pots are an amazing possibility for potatoes likewise. These growing containers are light-weight, environmentally friendly, and fabricated from cloth, therefore your potatoes get air as they grow. They even have a nice natural evacuation, making certain your potatoes can never sit in water and decay.

The Potting Soil

Use a fast draining and high-quality potting soil, particularly if you are using a plastic container. Organic soils are continually a decent alternative likewise. If you intend to use a good pot, you'll be able to use a garden soil mixed with compost.

The Fertilizer

Mix an organic fertilizer and slowly unleash it into the potting soil once you are planting your potatoes. Because the potatoes grow, it's a decent plan to use a diluted liquid fertilizer like fish emulsion each number of weeks.

Sun and Water

Potatoes won't grow well without adequate sun and water. Place your container wherever it'll receive a minimum of six to eight hours of sun each day.

Your potatoes additionally want consistent water and you'll get to be observant concerning maintaining an ideal balance. You would need to maintain a moist soil, however not wet. If the soil is just too dry, the plants can die; if it's too wet, the potatoes can rot. If the wetness level is inconsistent, your spuds are going to be deformed.

The nice factor concerning containers is that you will visibly see once you have watered deeply enough. Simply stay up for water to flow out of the container's bottom and you may notice if they need more quantity of water or not.

Adding Soil and Fertilizer

Now that you have all of your materials, it is time to plant your potatoes. Fill your container with a minimum of 4-6 inches of potting soil. If your soil doesn't embody a fertilizer, combine in a very slow-release plant food per the directions on the box.

One of the benefits of using an organic form of fertilizer is that it doesn't affect the plant if you mistakenly used it in excess, unlike the conventional fertilizer which could hurt your plants.

Preparing Potatoes for Growing

There are a couple of ways for making potatoes ready for planting and one isn't essentially higher than the other.

Some farmers await their potatoes to sprout and a few others simply plant them. Then, there are people who cut their potatoes and leave them for a couple of days to dry off before planting, while others simply cut the potatoes right before planting. If your potatoes are tiny, you ought not to cut them into bits as you can plant them as they are.

When you cut your potatoes, ensure that you.

- Cover Your Potatoes with Soil

After you've planted your seed potatoes, cover them with a handful of inches of soil and compost. Don't plant them too deep. 1-4 inches is ideal and also the cooler the climate, the less soil you should place on it.

Water your freshly planted potatoes well. Keep in mind that one of the keys to growing potatoes is keeping your soil moist, not wet. This can't be stressed enough.

- Check the container at least once daily

To visualize the wetness level, stick your finger a minimum of an inch into the soil (or up to your second knuckle). If it feels dry, it is time to water. Make sure you water deeply by watching closely until water begins to run out of the bottom. It's harmful to merely water the surface of the soil.

"Hilling" Your Potatoes as They Grow

Once your potato plants have grown up about six inches, you should "hill" them. This is often done by adding a handful of inches of soil and compost. Combine them around your potato plants. Be cautious not to break the plants while doing this.

You will be covering a number of the leaves of the plants likewise. The goal is to cover a small part of the plant (with its leaves) coming out of the soil.

Repeat the hilling method a couple of times as your plants grow. You'll be able to stop once the soil reaches the top of your container. Potato plants grow so fast, therefore, keep an eye fixed on them so that you can properly manage them.

Harvesting Your Potatoes

You can begin to reap potatoes anytime the plants have patterned. Rigorously reach down into the soil of your container and pull out a couple of potatoes at a time.

You can additionally wait till the plants flip yellow and shrink, then, harvest all of the potatoes right away. The simplest way to try this is to turn the container over, pouring it into a cart or onto a canvass. You'll be able to then freely paw through the soil to search out all of the potatoes.

You may realize a couple of very little potatoes, however do not wedge them. Those might be the sweetest potatoes of the year and they make a perfect stew recipe.

Cook your potatoes quickly or store them for later use. For storage, begin by brushing aside the dirt, then allow them to dry for few days. They are best kept in baskets or paper baggage that enable them to breathe.

CHAPTER TEN

HOW TO GROW CABBAGE IN CONTAINERS

Cabbage is a nice vegetable to mix in many meals. If you'd grow cabbage in pots in your vegetable patch, it might be easy to toss up a salad; embody it as an ingredient or steam it as a supplement to a meal. It doesn't need rocket science to grow cabbage in containers, though some information is useful.

If you would like to grow cabbage in containers, you initially have to be compelled to decide the variety you would like to grow and therefore the quantity of area you have is also important. Once that's done, you just need to follow the directions below to grow cabbage in pots.

THINGS TO THINK ABOUT WHEN GROWING CABBAGE IN CONTAINERS

- **Size of container**

To grow cabbage plants in pots, you need huge and spacious containers. This is because cabbage needs space for the roots to grow, and overcrowding can result in a poor yield. A decent rule of thumb for growing cabbage in pots is to limit your plants to at least one per 5-gallon container.

- **Style of Cabbage**

There's a large variety of cabbage that may be fully grown. The time of planting and spacing needed are going to be determined by the variability of cabbage you decide on planting.

- **Watering**

Cabbage plants need regular watering to grow well. Once you grow cabbage plants in pots they'll need a lot of watering than those growing in a garden. If it gets too hot as you grow cabbage in containers, you should mulch the plants to help prevent dryness.

- **Pests and Diseases**

There are common pests and diseases that

affect cabbage plants. As you grow cabbage plants in pots, it'll be simple to select off the pests and treat the diseases which will attack your crop like plant disease, deformity flora, and yellow virus. The pests embody cabbage worms, cutworms and cabbage loopers. To grow cabbage in pots, make sure the soil is healthy to avoid diseases that are sometimes carried within the soil.

- **Companion Plants**

Planting companion plants alongside your container cabbage plants can offer a natural remedy to pest management. A companion plant that may be enclosed as you grow cabbage in pots includes onions and herbs that makes it difficult for the pests to search out the cabbage as they need a robust scent that hides the scent of the cabbage plants.

How to Grow Cabbage in Containers

Cabbage is a nutritive vegetable, made of fibre and vitamins and low in calories. Growing cabbage in containers provides several advantages, particularly for gardeners who do not have much sunny garden area. Growing cabbage in containers is not difficult and only a little soil excavation is needed. To avoid the summer heat, plant cabbage in early spring or early time of year.

1. Purchase a cabbage transplant at a garden center or nursery. Choose from green cabbage varieties like "King Cole" or "Cheers" or red cabbages like "Ruby Ball" or "Red Meteor." Savoy cabbage, a cabbage with rippled, green leaves, is accessible in varieties like "Savoy Queen" or "Savoy King."

2. Fill a container with industrial potting soil containing ingredients like vegetable matter, compost and vermiculite. A container with a depth of twelve inches and a diameter of eighteen inches is large enough for one cabbage plant. Use a container with an evacuation hole.

3. Mix a slow-release chemical into the soil before planting. Use a balanced, granular chemical with an N: P: K magnitude like 13:13:13 or 14:14:14.

4. Dig a hole in the centre of the container. Plant the cabbage in the hole, deep enough that the second leaf is simply higher than the surface of the soil.

5. Put the soil firmly around the stem.

6. Place the container wherever the cabbage is exposed to daylight for a minimum of six hours per day.

7. Check the cabbage daily, as potting soil in containers dries quickly, particularly throughout hot weather. Poke your finger into the soil, and water whenever it feels dry. Water slowly until water trickles through the evacuation hole, then water once more when the soil feels dry.

8. Fertilize the cabbage a second time once the plants begin to make heads. Use a soluble NPK Fertilizer with a magnitude of 20-20-20. Combine the chemical in line with the recommendations on the label.

9. Cut the cabbage from the plant once the pinnacle feels firm and solid.

Things You Will Need

- Commercial potting soil

- Container with an evacuation hole

- Balanced slow-release chemical

- Balanced soluble chemical

CHAPTER ELEVEN

HOW TO GROW SPINACH IN CONTAINERS

Spinach is one of the easiest vegetables to grow in the shade and containers. It's an ideal container plant especially when you're short of outdoor space. You only need to purchase a few 6 inches deep small pots or look for a container of similar size to grow your spinach.

Spinach is naturally a cool season crop, but it's equally adaptable to hot seasons. It is quite easy to grow in the tropics and subtropics. While growing spinach in the hot summer months, you will need to water it regularly and provide it with enough shade in order to keep the soil temperature cool.

Another important thing to note while planting your spinach in the container is to choose your variety carefully as there are heat tolerant varieties which might be best for planting your spinach in a container. These varieties tolerate heat and humidity as they produce a high yield.

Growing Spinach in containers from Seeds

Sow seeds 1/2 inches deep directly in containers or a seed receptacle. Seedlings can germinate in 5-14 days depending on the variability of growing conditions. If you have a seed tray, wait till 2-3 true leaves appear on every plant, then transplant them into the first pots with care.

- **Choosing a pot**

For growing spinach in pots, select a pot that's at east 6-8 inches deep. You don't want an awfully deep pot. However, you can decide to use a large window box to plant all your spinach at once or make use of many small pots to grow your spinach plant.

- **Spacing**

Provide every Spinach plant with an area of 3 inches. If you would like to choose giant leaves, offer extra space to every plant, 5 inches. If you would like to reap leaves at a tender age, then keep the spacing reduced to 2 inches.

Requirements for Growing Spinach in Containers

- **Position**

If you're growing spinach in fall (autumn), keep the plant in a very sunny spot (in delicate climates) owing to shorter days and low intensity of the sun. For spring and summer planting, keep your potted plants in a location where it will receive some shade, particularly in the afternoon. In hot weather climate, place your spinach containers in a spot where it would get much shade.

- **Soil**

For growing spinach in containers, use quality potting combination made in the organic matter. The feel of the soil should be breakable and loamy. Avoid soil that clogs the drainage and remains wet. Well-draining soil is a vital issue for the optimum growth of spinach in containers. Soil pH should be neutral.

- **Watering**

You need to avoid stagnant water when growing spinach in containers as this could cause rot and predispose it to several other fungal diseases.

Also, avoid wetting the foliage. Keep the soil dampish, however not soggy or wet. Taking care of fine drainage within the pot is critical.

- **Temperature**

Spinach seeds germinate in temperatures as low as 40°F and in high temperatures too. The most effective soil temperature for growing spinach falls within the range of 50-80°F.

- **Spinach Care**

Growing spinach in pots doesn't need too much special care. Regular watering, fertilizing and getting the right soil are the key to a good harvest.

- **Fertilizing**

Nitrogen is essential for growing healthy green spinach. At the time of planting, you'll be able to combine time-based fertilizer, otherwise you will add plenty of compost or well-rotted manure, and this can give nutrients slowly. Feeding the plant with fish emulsion, compost or manure tea within the middle of the expansion could be a nice organic remedy for the plants. If you've not added time-based fertilizer, you should rather feed the plant with balanced liquid fertilizer at regular intervals.

- **Mulching**

Although you're growing spinach in pots, do mulching. Mulching plants with organic matter can help to retain much water in the soil.

- **Pests and Diseases**

You don't have to be bothered about pests as you're growing spinach in containers; this is because you will be able to easily manage them. However, you need to keep a close watch on leaf-eating insects such as caterpillars and slugs.

- **Harvesting**

Spinach is prepared for harvest 37-50 days after germination depending on the growing conditions and variety.

Harvesting is done once the plant has produced a minimum of 5-6 healthy leaves, and is a minimum of 3-4 inches long. Harvest the outer leaves and leave the new inner leaves in order so that they can grow or cut the total plant off at the bottom with a knife. Once it is not completely uprooted, it will definitely sprout once more.

CONCLUSION

Gardening has never been so interesting like you have it when you start a container vegetable farm. All the tips written in this book are here for you to know how to start up your vegetable farm.

So, if you are here reading the conclusion of this book, it shows that you have thoroughly read through this book and learned some DIY tips that will help you become a better vegetable farmer.

Perhaps you clicked the conclusion, and you got here without reading the content, you should read it.

By now you will agree that it's quite easy to plant the vegetable of your choice at home by simply following the simple steps highlighted in this book. Understanding and practicing all the steps of planting your vegetable is a key to improved health as vegetables have lots of health benefits.

Planting your favorite vegetables is a great way to save money as you can simply harvest your vegetables whenever you want to eat it. Once proper vegetable management practice is in place, you will be able to have your favorite vegetables available all year round. Start planting and consuming more of vegetables in your diet and see how your health dramatically improves.

You do not have any other excuse not to plant vegetables as it could be planted right in a container at your home. Once you take note of the steps highlighted in this book such as your choice of vegetable variety, watering, fertilizer application and how to harvest, you will have a successful vegetable farm. With the right harvesting technique, you can maintain a constant vegetable harvest. There is no better time to start your container vegetable garden than now.

-------***STEVE MUFIA***

Check Out Other Books

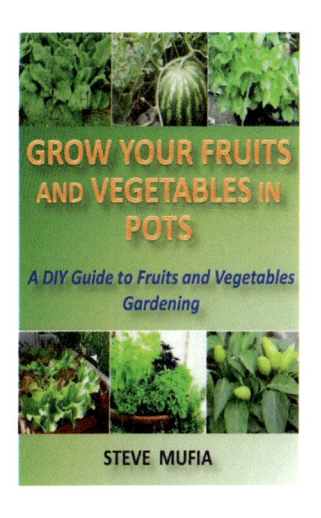

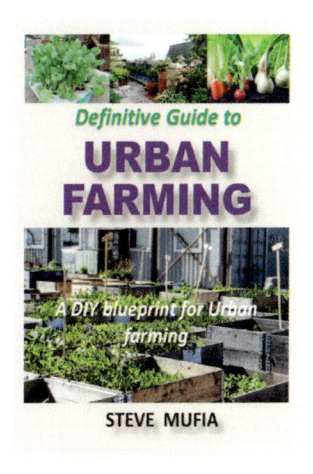

Raised Bed Gardening

A DIY Guide to Raised Bed Gardening

STEVE MUFIA

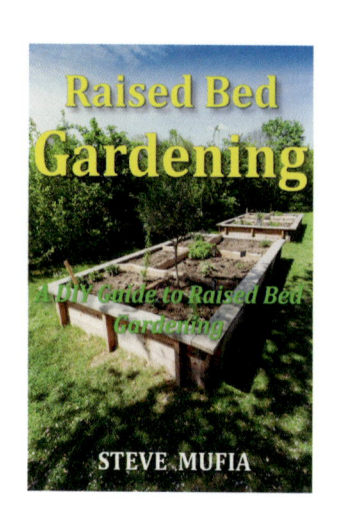

Printed in Poland
by Amazon Fulfillment
Poland Sp. z o.o., Wrocław